IMAGES
of America

DOVER AIR
FORCE BASE

IMAGES
of America

DOVER AIR
FORCE BASE

Brig. Gen. Kennard R. Wiggins Jr. (DE ANG Retired)

ARCADIA
PUBLISHING

Copyright © 2011 by Brig. Gen. Kennard R. Wiggins Jr. (DE ANG Retired)
ISBN 978-0-7385-8212-2

Published by Arcadia Publishing
Charleston, South Carolina

Printed in the United States of America

Library of Congress Control Number: 2010937905

For all general information, please contact Arcadia Publishing:
Telephone 843-853-2070
Fax 843-853-0044
E-mail sales@arcadiapublishing.com
For customer service and orders:
Toll-Free 1-888-313-2665

Visit us on the Internet at www.arcadiapublishing.com

This book is dedicated to all the men and women who have served their country at Dover Air Force Base and to the unswerving support of the people of the city of Dover, Delaware.

CONTENTS

ACKNOWLEDGMENTS

This is my third book of military history for Arcadia Publishing, and I am grateful for the opportunity to have this much fun. Its team is extraordinary in every respect, and I appreciate, in particular, the guidance of my editor, Elizabeth Bray.

Thanks to Carl Butterworth, who first got me interested in the heritage of Dover Air Force Base. It has a fascinating history, and I was very fortunate to be granted access to the resources needed to research this project. Mike Leister, the director of the Air Mobility Museum at Dover, made sure that I was given the full measure of cooperation and support from the museum archives. His infectious enthusiasm for this place was shared by Harry Heist, the museum archivist and resident human encyclopedia. I am also grateful for the technical support of John Taylor, the operations manager. The museum would not exist without the effort of its scores of dedicated volunteers who humble me with their efforts. I share an appreciation with thousands of current and former members of this storied organization, their families, friends, and neighbors. Many more than I can count, or can find room to name here, have demonstrated their dedication by adding bits to the history of the Dover Air Force Base. They have offered their stories, photographs, and personal experiences over a period of decades to accumulate this history. Their history documents tireless dedication, personal integrity, service before self, and excellence in all that they do.

I end with a final note of appreciation to my good friend and neighbor, Van Templeton, who was my partner on this project. Van dedicated numberless hours commuting to Dover with me and scanning literally hundreds of images, halving the time this task would have ordinarily taken. Everyone should be so lucky as to have a sidekick like Van.

All photographs in this book are courtesy of the Dover Air Force Base Air Mobility Command Museum except as otherwise noted.

INTRODUCTION

Dover Air Force Base is the centerpiece of Kent County, Delaware, and is the county's largest employer. It has international significance as the nation's largest aerial port for military aerial cargo and is daily engaged in supporting overseas efforts to secure the nation's defense. It also serves humanitarian needs, bringing relief to victims of floods, earthquakes, storms, and other natural and man-made calamities around the globe. Delawareans for generations have driven past the base and marveled at the giant transport aircraft based there, but few know the story of the base's growth and development during the past decades. This book attempts to offer a history of Dover Air Force Base from its beginnings as an Army Air Corps training field to the sprawling complex that exists today.

The city fathers of Dover took a gamble in 1940 when they purchased nearby farmland in the corporate limits of the town to build a municipal airport whose construction would be funded by federal money. They did not know it at the time, but it would be the wisest investment the city ever made. The airport opened only a week after Pearl Harbor and promptly was federalized for the war emergency. At the time, it consisted of a star-shaped series of runways and the foundation for a hangar.

During World War II, the base served three purposes. Initially, it was a base for antisubmarine patrols offshore at the Delaware capes. The base was closed for a period in 1943 and was enlarged to accommodate the training of P-47 fighter pilots for the duration of the war. Finally, it served as a secret test facility for aerial rockets. Like many similar bases, Dover was mothballed immediately after World War II. It might have faced oblivion but was reopened for the Korean conflict.

Dover resumed its role as a fighter training base briefly until it was marked as a strategic location for military airlift by Air Force leadership. In 1953, the 1607th Air Base Wing was organized, and airlift missions began with C-54 Skymasters, followed by giant C-124 Globemaster IIs the next year. The Military Air Transport Service directed Dover aircraft for airlift missions to Europe, supporting deployments and exercises stateside, and to the Arctic, with an occasional Pacific Rim airlift as well. The focus, however, was to be, and remain, the East Coast, European, and Middle East routes.

The base population grew, and the supporting facilities that were constructed made ever-widening ripples in the local economy. Dover, although it was the state capital, was nevertheless a sleepy small town until the arrival of the base. Civic pride and a growing population of Air Force retirees and dependents made a huge impact upon the local economy.

For the past half-century and more, Dover has witnessed almost continuous growth as the aircraft and supporting facilities expanded to make the mission capability more responsive. The C-133 Cargomaster planes yielded to the jet age C-141 Starlifter, the C-5 Galaxy, and the latest C-17 Globemaster III successively.

The raison d'être of Dover AFB is to provide the strategic airlift of personnel, materiel, and equipment. But it is almost equally known for its port mortuary. The Charles C. Carson Center for Mortuary Affairs is the largest in the Department of Defense (DoD) and plays a vital role as a place of honor where the remains of DoD personnel killed overseas are received. It has processed the remains of the victims of the terrorist attacks on the USS *Stark*, the USS *Cole*, the Marine barracks bombing in Beirut, and casualties from wars in Vietnam, Iraq, and Afghanistan, to name just some of its activities.

Another institution that is destined to bring recognition to Dover for decades to come is the Air Mobility Museum. Housed in historic hangar 1301, which was the former rocket testing facility, the museum has a dual mission to preserve and protect the heritage of Dover AFB and the Air Mobility Command (AMC) mission. The AMC is a major command of the US Air Force. Its mission is to deliver maximum war-fighting and humanitarian effects for America through rapid and precise global air mobility. The Air Mobility Command Museum is a part of the National Museum of the United States Air Force's field museum system. Today, the museum has more than 20,000 square feet of interior exhibit space, a theater, museum store, library, image archive, artifact storage area, and administration offices. It features a commemorative park and, above all, a superb collection of military planes, specializing in transport aircraft. It is a growing collection that at the time of this writing contains some 27 aircraft.

Today, Dover AFB covers more than 3,900 acres, has two runways, and 1,700 buildings. Capital assets and aircraft-related equipment add $5.8 billion to the value of America's defense resources assigned there. The base supports 18 tenant units both on and off base. It has an economic impact of more than $470 million on the local economy and ranks as Delaware's third-largest industry.

There are more than 4,200 military, 1,200 civilians, and 2,500 reservists who work at Dover AFB. They are actively involved in a variety of off-base activities, and a strong base-community program provides a forum and the spirit for military and civilian cooperation at all levels.

One

WORLD WAR II

Dover Air Force Base originated as a municipal airfield for the city of Dover, encouraged by the Civil Aeronautics Administration and funded with federal money on the eve of World War II. It opened for business the week following the attack on Pearl Harbor, although construction was incomplete, consisting of only runways and the foundation for a hangar. It was quickly federalized for the duration of the war.

The base served three major functions during World War II. It was first an antisubmarine base, serving as a platform for the Ohio National Guard 0-46 observation planes. This capacity was supplanted by DB-7s and B-25s in the same mission flown by the 45th Bombardment Group until March 1943, when the units transferred and the mission ceased while the base closed for renovations.

The renovations were to accommodate seven squadrons of P-47 fighters whose assignment during the next three years was to provide the final combat flying training for pilots destined for overseas assignments. The initial effort was to train Operational Training Units (OTU). Three squadrons of the 365th Fighter Group participated in getting up to standard as a unit and then shipping out. Later, four squadrons of the 312th Army Air Corps Base Unit were used as Replacement Training Units (RTUs) to train individuals as backfill replacements for units already posted overseas.

The third mission during the war was to conduct testing of aerial rockets on a wide variety of aircraft in a secret facility on the most remote part of the base. The responsible organization was the 4146th Base Unit. Everything from light liaison aircraft to medium bombers to the latest jet fighters was tried out as platforms for these stand-off weapons.

After Victory in Europe Day (VE Day) on July 1, 1945, Dover Army Airfield became a pre-separation processing center under the 125th Base Unit until its inactivation in September. Recruitment was added to the base's mission on September 30, 1945. The 618th Air Service Squadron was established to redeploy returning veterans, though it disbanded in November 1945. On September 1, 1946, Dover Army Air Field went on inactive status, and its personnel were reassigned to other commands.

A cartoon commentary of the ambitious undertaking in the sleepy state capital of Dover, Delaware, is copied from a local newspaper at the time.

A civilian farm property is depicted here in 1943 before its condemnation for Dover Air Force Base expansion.

A military police sentry guards the base from his primitive guard shack. The shack was evidently too small for an indoor stove.

Base housing for the 39th Bombardment Squadron is shown here in August 1942. The soldiers ate from their mess kits and bathed at civilian facilities.

Hangar 295 and its accompanying sea of mud are depicted in December 1942, just after the base opened.

Identified only by their last names, airmen Lunsford, Wolford, and Crowder, from the 3rd Antisubmarine Squadron, depart the Squadron Orderly Room in 1942. The tar paper shacks at Dover were little different from hastily improvised overseas air patches in the combat zone. Heated by potbellied stoves, the early occupants had no running water or electricity.

This aircraft was part of the 112th Observation Squadron, Ohio National Guard, North American O-47 Owl. What is thought to be the only remaining O-47B (serial no. 39-112) is on display at the National Museum of the United States Air Force at Wright-Patterson AFB near Dayton, Ohio. It is displayed in the markings of an O-47A belonging to the 112th Observation Squadron.

Barracks of the 3rd Antisubmarine Squadron are depicted in the winter of 1942. That winter, the heaviest rains in 12 years turned the facility into a quagmire. The property is very near the wetlands and marsh along Delaware Bay, and in heavy rains there was little to distinguish the field from marshes to the east.

A B-25 is shown here after a minor incident with a gully. The 39th Bombardment Squadron, also called the "Bat Out of Hell Squadron," arrived in July 1942 flying B-25 Mitchell Medium bombers. Both the 80th and 39th squadrons were part of the 45th Bombardment Group performing in the antisubmarine patrol mission. They provided aerial escort to merchant convoys and performed search and patrol for submarines. Note the "Bat Out of Hell Squadron" insignia on the starboard fuselage beneath the cockpit.

Maj. Alfred E. Bent, commanding officer of the 3rd Antisubmarine Squadron, poses before a B-24 bomber. Bent was an unlucky aviator. He was the pilot in two of the five recorded B-25 crashes of the 39th Bombardment Squadron in the autumn of 1942.

Base Operations is depicted here in 1943. It is a big improvement from the earlier tents and tar paper shacks and a step up from primitive field conditions.

A characteristic sign of the times is displayed at the Main Gate during wartime in October 1943. This is the Army Air Force equivalent of "loose lips sink ships."

The Base Personnel Office is shown in 1943. It was heated by potbellied stoves and ventilated by windows.

The barracks for most of the men were wooden, open-bay structures with racks of bunks arrayed side by side in rows. Housekeeping was stressed. Brass was to be polished, pipes painted, windowsills dusted, stones raked, cars parked properly, lawns policed of litter, and supplies stored neatly.

Republic P-47 Thunderbolts were built in greater quantities than any other US fighter. The P-47, also known as the "Jug," was the heaviest single-engine World War II fighter to go into production and the first piston-powered fighter to exceed 500 miles per hour. The Thunderbolt performed 546,000 combat sorties between March 1943 and August 1945.

The Base Quartermaster's Office included civilian employees from nearby Dover and was a boon to the local economy, providing jobs for the community.

A Dover Army Air Field aviator proudly poses next to his steed, a Vultee Valiant BT-13 Trainer.

The Base Fire House is shown in 1943. It provided crash trucks for flight line aircraft incidents as well as structural fires. The firehouse was among the earliest buildings erected on base.

(Q-4)(3-10-43-1200)(f/82 open flash)(Officers' Mess-Dover A.B. - DELA.)

Shown here in 1943, the officers' mess was the main dining facility for commissioned officers.

Rehoboth - 1944

Bernice Souza

Bernice Souza, head nurse, is photographed on summer furlough from Dover AFB at Rehoboth Beach, a popular destination for Dover personnel.

The Dover Army Air Forces baseball team compiled a 22-1 record in the Lower Delaware League in 1944; however, they lost the championship to the Fort Miles artillery team in the season playoffs.

Physical fitness training for the student pilots and staff was part of the regular wartime routine.

The obstacle course was considered a key part of the fitness training regimen for soldiers who might later be faced with escape and evasion procedures in enemy territory.

The enlisted mess was the primary dining facility for soldiers with big appetites.

The base canteen provided coffee, snacks, and the equivalent of fast food for hungry soldiers. The insignia hanging on the walls shown in this picture still exist. They were rescued by a salvage buyer after the base closed and then donated to the base museum many years later.

Soldiers stand in queue at the base post office to mail parcels back home.

Shown here on the ramp at Dover Army Air Field in 1945, pilots ready themselves and their P-47s to train for combat before posting to overseas assignments.

A squadron party complete with tablecloth and finery for wives and girlfriends is depicted in this 1943 photograph.

The tar paper 1st Air Force, 125th Army Air Force Base Unit Headquarters Building is depicted in 1944. This humble structure, like many others, was destined for replacement during the building boom in the 1950s and 1960s.

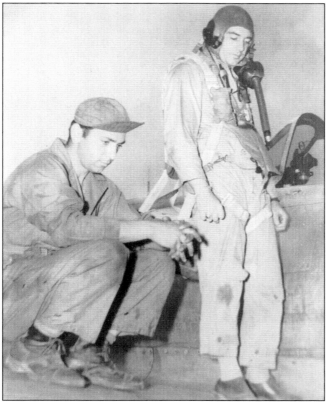

A pilot is prepared by his crew chief for flight while perched on the wing of their P-47.

At Dover, hundreds of Thunderbolt pilots received their final phase of training before posting overseas for combat duty. It was a hazardous enterprise. From August 1943 to April 1946, about 180 P-47s were involved in accidents around Dover, ranging from fender benders to fatal destruction.

Soldiers from Dover AFB march in a rainy-day parade in downtown Dover in 1944, probably during a war bond drive.

The Rocket Test Facility hangar, building 1301, was constructed in 1944 and is one of the very few structures from that era that still remains. It is now the Air Mobility Command Museum. The Delaware Bay is in the background to the east. In this picture, the visible aircraft are (clockwise from the lower left corner) a B-17, B-25, P-61, A-26, Culver PQ-1 Cadet, P-47, CQ-3, P-63, P-38, and another B-17.

A North American P-51D Mustang demonstrates a live-fire rocket test. The North American Aviation P-51 Mustang was a long-range, single-seat World War II fighter aircraft. Designed and built in just 117 days, the Mustang first flew in the Royal Air Force as a fighter-bomber and reconnaissance aircraft before converting to a bomber escort that employed in raids over Germany, helping ensure Allied air superiority from early 1944.

The Martin B-26 Marauder was tested as a rocket platform. It was a World War II twin-engine medium bomber built by the Glenn L. Martin Company. The first US medium bomber used in the Pacific theater in early 1942, it was also used in the Mediterranean theater and in Western Europe. A total of 5,288 were produced between February 1941 and March 1945.

A Republic P-47 Thunderbolt sports a very large rocket mounted under the wing in this photograph. Rockets were tested on almost every combat platform in the Air Force inventory at the secret Dover facility.

That is not a cannon in the nose; it is a rocket launcher with a rotary rack inside holding six five-inch rockets. This Douglas A-26 Invader was modified for rocket-testing by the 4146th Base Unit.

This P-40N was piloted by Herman F. Boyd of the 4146th Base Unit in this photograph taken on February 2, 1945. The plane ran out of fuel on takeoff.

The Bell P-63 Kingcobra was tested as a rocket-launcher platform. The Kingcobra (Model 24) was developed in World War II from the P-39 Airacobra in an attempt to improve that aircraft's deficiencies. Although the aircraft was not accepted for combat use by the US Army Air Forces, it was successfully adopted by the Soviet Air Force as part of the Lend-Lease program.

A Republic P-47 Thunderbolt displays its underwing rockets for the camera.

Shown here is a North American B-25 Mitchell that has been fitted with rocket launchers outboard of the engines. The B-25 Mitchell was an American twin-engine medium bomber manufactured by North American Aviation. It was used by many Allied air forces in every theater of World War II, as well as many other air forces after the war ended, and it saw service across four decades.

The Stinson L-5 Sentinel liaison/spotter plane began life as the prewar model 105 built by the Stinson division of Consolidated Vultee. When World War II broke out, the Voyager was redesigned and then entered into service as a liaison aircraft. It also flew in the artillery spotter role and as an air ambulance. Testing revealed that the rocket exhaust had an unfortunate tendency to burn the fabric wings.

The Douglas A-26 Invader (B-26 between 1948 and 1965) was a twin-engine light attack bomber built by the Douglas Aircraft Company during World War II that also saw service during several of the Cold War's major conflicts. A limited number of highly modified aircraft served in combat until 1969. The redesignation of the type from A-26 to B-26 has led to eternal confusion with the Martin B-26; they are completely different designs.

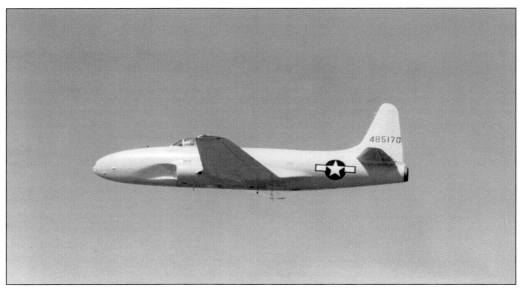

The arrival in January 1946 of the Lockheed P-80 jet fighter caused quite a stir. The base newspaper, the *Dover Blast*, featured the new jet as the wave of the future and predicted future air travel would rely upon jet engines. The P-80 was sent to Dover AFB for aerial rocket testing. It was the first operational jet in the flying inventory of the US Army Air Forces and saw extensive combat in Korea with the US Air Force as the F-80.

A Boeing B-29 Superfortress and its smaller companion, an AQ-8 Drone, pose on the flight line at Dover AFB.

A Douglas A-20 Havoc tow plane from the 13th Tow Target Squadron and its underslung towing target are prepared for flight in 1943.

On Victory in Europe Day in May 1945, an unidentified member of the 125th Army Air Force Base Unit posts "Das Reich ist kaput" on a map of Germany.

A cartoon depicted from the January 26, 1945, issue of the *Dover Blast* reads, "They Keep 'em Flying" with sketches by Cpl. Bob Johnston.

Two

TENANT UNITS

Dover Air Force Base has been a major center for the US Air Force's global airlift mission for more than half a century, but it has served many other functions as well. This chapter showcases those other missions mostly performed by "tenant" units. Echoing the World War II training experience, the 336th Fighter-Interceptor Squadron, the "Rocketeers," was posted to the recently renamed Dover Air Force Base from August to November in 1950 while training for combat in Korea with F-86 Sabrejets.

Dover is a strategic location on the East Coast close to the population centers of the nation's capital, Baltimore, Philadelphia, and New York. For many years, fighter-interceptors based at Dover were charged with defending the skies over these important cities.

The first organization to fly the air-defense mission was the Pennsylvania Air National Guard 148th Fighter-Interceptor Squadron, which used F-51s, F-84Cs, and F-94s during the Korean War. They were relieved in November 1952 by the 46th Fighter-Interceptor Squadron, which flew F-94s. They were joined in March 1956 by the 98th Fighter Squadron flying F-89 Scorpions and later F-101B Voodoos. In September 1963, the 98th was relieved by the 95th Fighter-Interceptor Squadron "Boneheads," which used F-106 Delta Daggers.

Other subsidiary functions included aerial refueling of Strategic Air Command Bombers performed by the 11th Air Refueling Group flying KC-97s in the early 1960s, air rescue, ferrying operations, and serving as a base for transient aircraft. To airmen, Dover was an aerial crossroads between European and domestic traffic. As a result, many famous visitors have graced the portals over the years, including presidents, entertainers, and heroes. Count Basie, Guy Lombardo, Rod Serling, and Katie Harmon, who was Miss America 2002, are just a few examples of the luminaries who have passed through Dover Air Force Base.

A C-46 Curtis Commando transport perches on the ramp during a base open house on June 10, 1945, as victorious P-47s soar past in formation in celebration of victory over Germany. The C-46 was later based at Dover as part of the 1607th Air Base Group from 1955 to 1957.

Shown here is a Beechcraft C-45 Expeditor light transport liaison aircraft. The C-45 was used by the 125th Base Unit from 1944 to 1946 and by the 1607th Air Base Group from 1952 to 1959. A trainer variant, the AT-7 Navigator, was based at Dover from 1949 to 1951.

In December 1948, the Army transferred the base to the Continental Air Command (CONAC). This command utilized the Douglas C-47 until February 18, 1949, when it transferred to the Ninth Air Force. The base was host to National Guard units for summer training during this period of relative inactivity.

The C-47 was also used as a utility aircraft by the 1607 Air Base Group from 1949 to 1961.

In 1951, the federalized 148th Fighter-Interceptor Squadron of the Pennsylvania Air National Guard was assigned to Dover flying F-51 Mustangs. During its tenure at Dover, the squadron transitioned to Republic F-84C Thunderjets, then F-94B and F-94C Starfire interceptor aircraft, such as the F94-C here firing rockets during a training exercise.

Lt. Col. W.J. O'Donnell of the 46th Fighter-Interceptor Squadron (FIS) poses by his F-94. In November 1952, the 46th Fighter-Interceptor Squadron, 4709th Air Defense Wing relieved the demobilized Pennsylvania Air Guard 148th FIS in the interceptor role at Dover Air Force Base. The squadron also flew F-94 Starfires. Its job was to "stay aware and counter any attack by the 'Russian Bear.'"

Pictured is an F-94 of the 46th Fighter-Interceptor Squadron. Note the black saber-toothed tiger emblem on the fuselage. The Lockheed F-94 Starfire was the Air Force's first operational jet-powered, all-weather interceptor aircraft. It was a redesign by the Lockheed Corporation of the twin-seat T-33 Shooting Star trainer aircraft.

The 46th Fighter-Interceptor Squadron maintained four F-94s of its 20 assigned aircraft on 24-hour alert, keeping them "cocked and loaded" for an airborne launch within five minutes. The 46th remained at Dover AFB until July 1, 1958.

The reconstituted and redesignated 98th Fighter-Interceptor Squadron was activated at Dover AFB on March 8, 1956, as a component of the Air Defense Command and was assigned to the 4709th Air Defense Wing, Eastern Air Defense Force.

An F-101B of the 98th Fighter Squadron banks over Governor's Island, New York City, in the performance of its mission to guard and defend America's skies.

Through a change in command, the 98th Fighter Squadron was assigned to the New York Air Defense Sector. In March 1959, the squadron converted to the supersonic McDonnell F-101B Voodoo Interceptors. The 98th remained until September 30, 1963, when it were relieved by the 95th Fighter Squadron, also known as the "Boneheads."

An all-weather McDonnell F-101B Voodoo interceptor armed with two MB-2 Genie nuclear-tipped air-to-air missiles is shown on static display at a base open house. Air-to-air nuclear missiles are no longer in the Air Force inventory of weapons.

This undated photograph shows Red Cross volunteers and nurses at an unknown location. The volunteers were mostly dependents of Air Force service members.

Young airmen report for mail call in 1964 to receive mail from home.

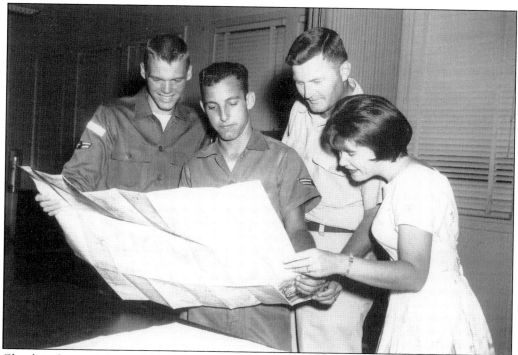

Chaplain Stuart E. Barstad (third from left) joins chapel staff members at Chapel One in 1964 in this photograph. Chaplain Barstad retired as a major general and USAF chief of chaplains.

Dover airmen take a break from their labors to get caught up on the news in the weekly base newspaper, the *Airlifter*, on the steps of their barracks.

The first F-106 Delta Dart arrived at Dover AFB on August 3, 1963, as part of the fleet of the newly assigned 95th Fighter-Interceptor Squadron, the Boneheads. The all-weather Convair F-106 interceptor first flew in 1956. It could counter bomber attacks to 70,000 feet at a maximum speed of 1,525 miles per hour (Mach 2.3) with a range of 1,500 miles. The Dart carried four Falcon missiles and a Genie nuclear rocket.

Some 55 F-106s were assigned to the 95th Fighter-Interceptor Squadron at two different locations: Andrews Air Force Base in Maryland from July 17, 1959, to July 1, 1963, and Dover Air Force Base in Delaware from July 1, 1963 (including Detachment 1 at Atlantic City), until its inactivation on January 31, 1973.

The Boneheads manned the 24-hour alert interceptor mission defending the Washington, DC, area and were assigned to the New York Air Defense Sector (1963–1966), the 21st Air Division (1966–1969), and the 20th Air Division (1969–1973). They deployed to Osan Air Base in South Korea from November 15, 1969 to May 1, 1970.

The 95th Fighter Interceptor Squadron stood down on January 31, 1973, and was transferred to Tyndall Air Force Base, where it converted to a training mission utilizing T-33s. The F-106 aircraft were reassigned to the 177th Fighter-Interceptor Group of the Atlantic City, New Jersey, Air National Guard. Thus ended the last combat fighter mission unit at Dover AFB, which henceforth became exclusively an airlift base of operations.

The first of 21 KC-97 Air Refueling aircraft arrived at Dover AFB on May 31, 1960, led by Col. Gilmer E. Walker Jr. Assigned to the 11th Air Refueling Squadron, the unit consisted of approximately 630 personnel.

The KC-97 was an aerial refueling tanker variant of the C-97 Stratofreighter, which was itself based on the B-29 Superfortress, and was greatly modified with all the necessary tanks, plumbing, and "flying boom." The cavernous upper deck was capable of accommodating oversize cargo accessed through a very large right-side door, and transferable jet fuel was contained in tanks on the lower deck.

The 11th Air Refueling Squadron supported Strategic Air Command B-52s and B-47s outside normal air traffic lanes in the Atlantic and Southeastern United States. The 11th Air Refueling Squadron remained at Dover until June 25, 1965, when it was posted at Altus Air Force Base in Oklahoma.

A KC-97G of the 11th Air Refueling Squadron was christened *Diamond State* during an annual open house in honor of its host state.

A single HH-43 Huskie was assigned to Dover from 1959 to 1962 with Detachment 48, Eastern Air Rescue Service (EARS).

The Huskie was used primarily for crash rescue and aircraft firefighting. It was in use with the US Navy when delivery of the H-43As to the US Air Force Tactical Air Command began in November 1958.

Pres. Dwight D. Eisenhower (left) and Delaware governor Caleb Boggs deplane the presidential airplane *Columbine* in June 1954 for a visit to Dover. Pres. Bill Clinton toured the base during a 1996 ceremony for deceased commerce secretary Ron Brown, and Pres. Barack Obama made a late-night visit in 2009 to honor war casualties.

Pres. Lyndon B. Johnson and Lady Bird Johnson arrive at Dover AFB on October 31, 1964, en route to a speaking engagement in the city of Dover. About 5,000 base military and civilian personnel and dependents were at the terminal to greet them, and another 10,000 awaited their arrival in downtown Dover.

Sen. John F. Kennedy landed at Dover AFB on June 22, 1960, and visited Delaware's Democratic delegates and newsmen at the Dover Hotel. US congressman Pierre S. DuPont IV toured Dover AFB on September 5, 1974.

Sen. Barry Goldwater is greeted by Dover airmen on a visit during the 1964 presidential campaign. Goldwater was a World War II veteran who retired with the rank of major general in the Air Force Reserve.

Legendary Tokyo raider Lt. Gen. Jimmy Doolittle (Retired) and his wife, Josephine, visited the base on May 6 and 7, 1982. Other famous aviators to visit include then Chief of Staff of the US Air Force Gen. Ron Fogleman, during a memorial ceremony for victims of the Khobar Towers terrorist attack in Dhahran, Saudi Arabia, in 1996, and Medal of Honor recipient John L. Levitow, who spoke to Airman Leadership class graduates at Dover AFB in 1997.

On April 18, 1998, Col. Gail Halverson (Retired) relived his role as the Berlin Airlift "Candy Bomber" when he dropped candy with attached parachutes from a C-54 over Dover AFB. This event kicked off the base's celebration commemorating the 50th anniversary of the Berlin airlift.

Astronaut Gus Grissom is greeted by the Base Leadership Team as he pays a visit to Dover AFB while on a training flight in a NASA T-38.

DuPont Company executives pose for the camera while on a VIP tour of the new C-124s in June 1954.

Miss Delaware 1964 Anita Gail Eubank is briefed by a 95th Fighter-Interceptor Squadron pilot during her visit to Dover AFB.

Miss Delaware 1969 Margo Ewing receives a tour of an airlifter during a visit to the base.

Pictured here in 1951 is communications officer Lieutenant Bracken, of the 148th Fighter Interceptor Squadron. He was the brother of actor Eddie Bracken.

The XC-99 was briefly based at Dover AFB in 1955 for testing and evaluation. It flew six missions to Keflavik, Iceland, in May. The Convair XC-99 (43-52436) was a prototype heavy cargo aircraft built by Convair for the US Air Force. It was the largest piston-engine land-based transport aircraft ever built and was developed from the B-36 bomber, sharing with it the wings and some other structures. Its first flight was in 1947 in San Diego and after testing it was delivered to the Air Force in 1949.

The CH-3 "Jolly Green Giant" helicopter was based at Dover in 1967, assigned to the 1042nd Test Squadron. The CH-3 was a twin-engine heavy-lift helicopter able to carry 25 combat-equipped troops, 15 litter patients for Medevac, or 5,000 pounds of cargo. Its crew consisted of a pilot, copilot, and flight engineer, with a parachute specialist and/or flight surgeon, depending on the mission.

The original star pattern of three runways is evident in this 1948 photograph of Dover AFB.

Three

A PERMANENT MISSION

At the conclusion of the Korean War, Dover Air Force Base might have once again been shuttered and eventually closed like so many other surplus properties of the Air Force. However, the Military Air Transport Service (MATS) recognized its strategic location on the East Coast as a point of embarkation and a foreign clearing base in April 1952. In a little more than a year, four support units of the MATS Atlantic Division set up on the base and became the nucleus that formed the 1607th Air Transport Wing (ATW).

Beginning with a medium airlift mission utilizing C-54G Skymasters, the base began airlift operations to overseas locations in November 1953. On May 1, 1954, the first C-124 Globemaster II aircraft was assigned to Dover AFB. The double-decker Globemaster II affectionately known as "Old Shaky" was the giant workhorse of its time, serving until the early 1960s.

The first C-133A (No. 54-0143) arrived at Dover on August 28, 1957, and was officially accepted by Military Air Transport Service commander Lt. Gen. Joseph Smith. This turboprop airlifter carried twice the useful load of its predecessor, the C-124, but was plagued by structural problems. During the 1950s and into the mid-1960s, the base played host to three C-54 squadrons, five C-124 squadrons, two C-133 squadrons, and two C-141 squadrons along with a ferrying squadron.

All this flying activity engendered nearly constant construction of facilities to support the mission. The collection of tar paper shacks from World War II was slowly replaced by more permanent infrastructure, including a new headquarters, maintenance shops, hangars, ramps, and runways.

The base added population to eventually total some 9,000 airmen and officers as well as 500 civilian employees in an area covering approximately 2,000 acres. Construction for a new and improved hospital, base schools, housing, a chapel, a base exchange, and commissary followed this boom.

The 1st Air Transport Squadron and the 21st Air Transport Squadron were reconstituted in September 1953 and activated on November 18, 1953, at Dover Air Force Base in Delaware as part of the 1607th Air Base Group. It was redesignated as "medium" and formed the nucleus of the new group. The "medium" classification referred to its mission aircraft, the Douglas C-54G Skymaster, which it flew until 1955.

Three more squadrons of airlifters were added in early 1954. On February 16, 1954, the 39th Air Transport Squadron (ATS) and the 45th ATS were assigned to the 1607 Air Transport Wing (ATW) and became operational in March. The 39th was redesignated "medium" and flew the Douglas C-54G Skymaster aircraft, mostly to Rhein-Main Air Base in Germany.

On May 1, 1954, the first C-124 Globemaster II aircraft was assigned to Dover AFB. The Douglas C-124 Globemaster II, known as Old Shaky, was a heavy-lift cargo aircraft built by the Douglas Aircraft Company in Long Beach, California.

First deliveries of the 448 production aircraft began in May 1950 and continued until 1955. The C-124 was the primary heavy-lift transport for US Air Force Military Air Transport Service (MATS) during the 1950s and early 1960s until the C-141 Starlifter entered service.

The 40th Air Transport Squadron was added to the rolls on March 8, 1954. It and the 45th ATS were redesignated "heavy," indicating they would take the Douglas C-124 Globemaster II as their mission aircraft. Reassigned to the 1607th Air Transport Group, on January 1, 1954, the 1st Airlift Squadron was redesignated 1st Air Transport Squadron, Heavy, on September 8, 1954. That same year, the unit added the C-124 to its aircraft inventory.

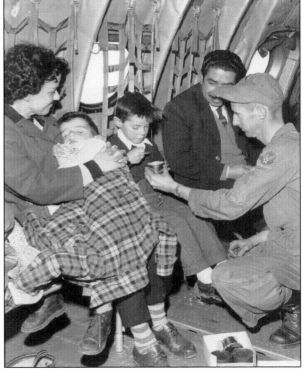

Crewman TSgt. Glenn A. Pecor comforts evacuated victims of the May 1960 Chilean earthquake. Named Operation Amigo Airlift, US Air Force Military Air Transport Service (MATS) flew 77 humanitarian missions to support the operation, including 33 Globemasters, allowing the wing to amass 1,700 flying hours. One minor accident resulted at Santiago when the main gear of a C-124 collapsed while taxiing to a stop. There were no injuries.

This cartoon illustrates some of the many problems airlift crews faced in the early days of strategic worldwide airlift. Bad weather, poor communications, maintenance problems, and primitive facilities faced aircrews as they pioneered such military transport around the globe.

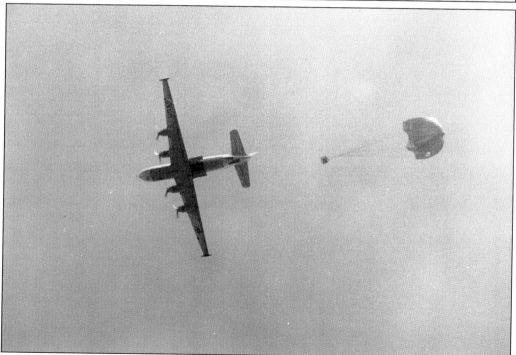

A 2,000-pound cargo bundle is delivered over the drop zone by a Dover C-124 Globemaster II during the Military Air Transport Service's annual aerial delivery competition at Fort Campbell, Kentucky.

The powerful Pratt and Whitney "Wasp Major" R-4360 engine powered the C-124. Each Wasp Major had 28 cylinders and produced some 3,800 horsepower. Unidentified Dover mechanics are depicted here performing routine maintenance on the engine.

A maintenance airman runs tests on the flight engineer panel in the cockpit of a C-124. All those dials monitor engine speed, temperature, manifold pressure, and more to ensure safe operation of the flight.

Refueling at Dover AFB was accomplished through underground systems built into the aircraft parking apron.

Unidentified aircrew members of the Douglas C-124 Globemaster II review flight plans while wheeled cargo is unloaded from the airplane.

An H-19 helicopter for the Air Rescue Service, partially disassembled, is loaded into a C-124C.

The Globemaster could lift almost anything that would fit into its giant maw, including this reflecting telescope mirror.

A C-124 Globemaster departed on April 18, 1962, from Dover carrying Col. John Glenn's space capsule, *Friendship VII*, to South America. All three of the wing's flying squadrons alternated escort duty during the worldwide tour culminating at the Seattle World's Fair on August 6, 1962. The wing also supported NASA by transporting the Gemini spacecraft in 1965.

A Dover AFB C-124 Globemaster is greeted by a bagpipe band in India during a humanitarian airlift mission.

Dogsleds still served a purpose at Fort Wainwright in Fairbanks, Alaska, during Exercise Polar Strike, the Army's midwinter maneuvers in January 1965. Military Air Transport Service C-124 Globemasters airlifted more than 6,000 troops and 5,000 tons of equipment for the exercise.

The Globemasters at Dover continued to set high marks during their tenure from 1954 to 1967. They flew 18-hour missions to French Morocco, lifted 24,000 pounds of priority cargo to Burtonwood, England, aided in the rescue of icebound passengers off Greenland, served as a temporary air-traffic control towers in Vietnam, and much more, according to base chronology.

This aerial photograph of Dover AFB around 1960 reveals the original star-shaped layout of the 1941 runway, altered, lengthened, and improved.

The modern 100-bed US Air Force hospital is shown here under construction. The facility went operational in May 1958.

The Transient Airmen's Quarters is depicted in 1957. This building serves as a home to enlisted airmen visiting Dover AFB on a temporary basis. M.Sgt. Harry Hettinger (Retired), an engine mechanic, noted this about the 1950s: "Back then it was three to a room in old World War II wooden constructions. Each barrack had one central latrine."

The Air Force began expanding what had been a relatively small Dover Air Force Base into a much larger transport center with a resulting increase in personnel and families and, for the Caesar Rodney School District, a sharp increase in base students. The first school on base was Dover Air Force Base School, which opened in 1961 and served students in grades 1 through 12.

Dover Air Force Base Elementary School was opened for the beginning of school in 1964. A year later a second, although smaller, elementary school was opened on base. Subsequently, the schools' names were changed to the current Major George S. Welch Elementary School and General Henry H. Arnold Elementary School, respectively.

The Dover Air Force Base Headquarters Building served as home to the administrative functions of the 1607th Air Transport Wing. A new personnel center was opened in December 1974. At about the same time, a new library was erected as well as an airmen dining hall.

Depicted here is the Dover Air Force Base Operations Center with the flight-line tower in the background on the aircraft parking ramp. The Operations Center served as a flight planning facility, and the tower served as a traffic direction for operations on the ground as well as a center for incoming and outgoing air traffic. A new air freight terminal was completed on November 30, 1974.

The base tower and ramp are in the foreground of this wide view of Dover Air Force Base. A 1607 Wing VT-29A is visible parked on the ramp.

The Dover Air Force Base Aero Club was a civilian facility for sport and recreational flying, as well as a place to offer flying lessons to base personnel. A bowling alley and a gymnasium were also part of the facilities to serve airmen and their dependents at Dover.

The base nondenominational chapel is depicted here in the early 1960s. Normally, Catholic, Protestant, and Jewish services were held here as well as christenings, weddings, and memorial services.

An interior view of the base chapel is depicted in this 1950s photograph. It was home to the base chaplain and provided a place for counseling, religious services, and ceremonies.

The Noncommissioned Officers' Club was opened in July 1958. An Airmen's Club was opened as part of the recreational center on February 22, 1974, and a youth center for dependents was completed in August 1974.

Like any small city, the base had a need for mail. The Dover Air Force Base Post Office served both official and dependent family needs.

The Dover Air Force Base Exchange Gasoline Station is depicted here in the 1950s. It was an on-base facility offering fuel at discounted prices for use by airmen and their dependent families. It later included facilities for washing, lubricating, and minor repair work.

The Dover Air Force Base Hobby Shop served the base population of airmen and dependents. It included a wood shop, automotive shop, photography, and arts and crafts as part of the support services for families on base. A recreation center was also on base for sports activities and for renting camping equipment. Off base, the personnel enjoyed the Fort Miles recreation complex at the Delaware shore.

A crowded view of the commissary around 1959 reveals Dover Air Force Base's explosive growth during the 1950s. According to Lt. Col. Harry Heist (Retired), "The Commissary was more of a small warehouse than a grocery store and was located to the west of the Skills Center."

The first C-133A (serial no. 54-0143) arrived at Dover on August 28, 1957, and was officially accepted by Military Air Transport Service commander Lt. Gen. Joseph Smith. The new Cargomaster flown by the 39th Air Transport Squadron (ATS) made the unit the first C-133A Squadron in the Air Force. The 39th ATS was activated on August 28, 1957. On September 8, 1957, it was redesignated 39th Air Transport Squadron, Heavy and finally as the 39th Military Airlift Squadron on January 8, 1966.

The Douglas C-133 Cargomaster was a large cargo aircraft built between 1956 and 1961 by the Douglas Aircraft Company. The C-133 was the Air Force's only production turboprop-powered strategic airlifter. It entered service shortly after Lockheed's better-known C-130 Hercules.

A tight fit and a heavy load, a US Army tank is disgorged from a C-133.

Civil Air Patrol cadets pose before a C-133 during their annual summer encampment in 1965.

Only 50 Cargomaster aircraft (32 C-133A and 18 C-133B) were constructed and put into service with the US Air Force. The plane provided airlift services in a wide range of applications and was replaced by the C-5 Galaxy in the early 1970s.

A C-133 dominates the ramp at Lajes Air Base in the Azores, which was a typical destination for Military Air Transport Service. Four C-133 aircraft departed Dover on July 5, 1964, marking the first time a scheduled around-the-world mission was ever attempted from Dover AFB using this model of aircraft.

This photograph illustrates the contrast between the size and loads carried on the C-133 Cargomaster (top) and the C-123 Provider aircraft (bottom). Both aircraft are represented at the Air Mobility Museum on Dover Air Force Base.

This photograph is an indication of the enormous size of the C-133. The wheel wells for the landing gear were nearly the size of a small aircraft.

A two-section rear door served as a loading ramp; the final three production models, however, featured clamshell doors allowing the aircraft to load and carry a Titan missile inside its 12-foot-high cargo bay.

The sleek tail of a C-133 poses near the tower during a base open house. Dover AFB assumed responsibility for all US Air Force C-133 pilot and flight engineer training on January 1, 1964.

Four

JET AIRLIFT

The global airlift mission assumed by Dover AFB was a demanding one. The technology that had already been applied to combat aircraft was adopted to airlift, resulting in jet-powered aircraft yielding ever more capability. The C-133 was a turbine-powered aircraft in use since 1957, but the first pure jet design was the C-141 Starlifter, which replaced the C-124 Globemaster II in 1965.

On December 27, 1965, the 436th Troop Carrier Wing was redesignated as the 436th Military Airlift Wing (MAW) and activated in conjunction with the creation of the Military Airlift Command. On January 8, 1966, the 436th MAW replaced the 1607th Air Transport Wing as the Military Airlift Command host wing at Dover Air Force Base. Shortly after its arrival at Dover, the 436th MAW began a transition into the jet age, replacing its propeller-driven C-124 Globemaster II aircraft with the jet-powered C-141 Starlifter.

In 1968, the 912th Military Airlift Group, Associate Reserve, was activated at Dover, giving the base a total of four active and one reserve military airlift squadrons. In 1973, the 512th Military Airlift Wing was activated as a replacement to the 912th and its subordinates. From 1971 to 1973, the transition was undertaken to make Dover home to the first all C-5–equipped wing in the Air Force.

The C-5 is the country's largest operational airlifter. Its arrival signaled another great round of military construction for ramps, hangars, and support facilities. It turned Dover AFB into the premier military aerial port in the United States. The wing received its first C-5B aircraft, tail number 85001, in August 1986.

The C-5 remained Dover's sole mission aircraft until the C-17 made its first appearance. The first C-17 Globemaster III aircraft arrived at Dover AFB on July 2, 2007. The base has 13 of these aircraft. The C-17s are assigned to the 436th Airlift Wing, and the 512th Airlift Wing provides a flying squadron and maintenance squadron to augment this mission. The inherent flexibility and performance of the C-17 force improves the ability of the total airlift system to fulfill the worldwide air mobility requirements of the United States.

The first C-141A Starlifter, named the *First State Starlifter*, was delivered to Dover AFB with arrival ceremonies attended by many state and local dignitaries on August 18, 1965.

This photograph contrasts the sleek lines and size of the jet-powered C-141 in the foreground with Old Shaky, a C-124, in the background. A transient T-38 trainer is at the middle left.

On September 18–19, 1965, a Dover AFB C-141A made its first long-distance overseas flight when it flew on a mission to Hickam Air Force Base in Hawaii.

This artful photograph is a close-up of the tall tail of the C-141. Another C-141 flies in the distance.

On April 28, 1973, Dover's C-141 Starlifter and aircrew made a historic flight to the People's Republic of China. This presidential-directed special airlift mission supported the newly established US Liaison Office in Peking.

Operations Desert Shield and Desert Storm became the focal point of airlift support in 1990, when the wing's two flying squadrons, the 326th and 709th Airlift Squadrons, were recalled to active duty. Also supporting the conflict were 232 maintenance personnel.

In this image, a fully assembled ballistic missile is loaded onto a C-141 for transport.

On February 16, 1970, Maj. Charles S. Gorton and crew brought a C-141 (serial no. 40610) to a safe, nose-gear–up landing on a cushion of foam with minimal damage.

In June 1971, the wing accomplished what no other Military Aircraft Command wing had ever done: flying 259 consecutive C-141 departures without a delay.

The Wing Reserve Associate Unit Program was implemented at Dover in 1968. The program was initiated by Gen. Howell M. Estes Jr., commander of Military Airlift Command (MAC). It permitted reservists to retain their unit identity and train with an active MAC wing carrying out the same operational and maintenance missions as equals with their active component counterparts.

Flying above the weather at 17,000 to 25,000 feet with no vibration and better radar and equipment, the C-141 was "a different world" after flying older transports, according to Lt. Col. Art Azamar, a master navigator who flew all the major transport planes: the C-54, C-124, C-133, C141, and the C-5A. Azamar said, "I thought I was in heaven after bouncing around for 10 years."

Young and old spectators are framed by the tail of a Starlifter at the popular annual base open house and air show.

An overhead view of the base open house is shown here in June 1987. The open house is an eagerly anticipated annual event that draws a crowd of tens of thousands.

The Dover Air Force Base Talent Team of 1984 includes, in no particular order, James Stanyard, Ken Huff, Darryl Bryant, Keith Coleman, Charles Cloud, Dale Dobrinski, James Hargett, William Kight, Paul Buckley, Carlos Holmes, Napolean Hutchinson, Tracy Humphrey, and John Taplin.

A base Brownie Troop politely poses for a group portrait, exemplifying "sugar and spice and everything nice."

In contrast with the previous photograph, a base Cub Scouts Pack enjoys a boisterous visit to Base Operations for an orientation, exemplifying "snips and snails and puppy dog tails."

Military Air Transport Service Youth Center trophy winners are pictured here in the Dover Air Force Base facility.

The swim team is instructed at the officers' club pool in 1964. Dover Air Force Base is comparable to a thriving community and a self-contained city serving the resident military and dependent population.

The Dover
Air Force Base
basketball team
poses for a
team portrait
in 1981 in the
base gymnasium.

The game ball is awarded to the 31st Air Transport Squadron softball team. Intramural sports
were a key ingredient of morale for assigned airmen.

The women's volleyball team poses for pictures at the Military Airlift Command Championship in 1988.

Two fashionable 1960s military dependents take pride in their "immortal driveway" with this inscrutable sign in the base housing area.

540-G-DAFB-27-SEP-57

A Dover AFB family housing project is photographed under construction in 1957. The second increment of the Capehart Family Housing Project started in October 1958.

Dover family housing typical of the 1960s is depicted here. About 500 units were constructed in the 1950s by Cape Constructors of Wilmington.

A multitude of fighter aircraft is visible at an annual base open house.

Dover AFB's first Women in the Air Force (WAF) squadron was activated as part of the 436th Air Base Group on September 1, 1970. 2nd Lt. Virginia Alden was appointed officer in charge of the 436th WAF squadron. Just five years later, in 1975, the squadron was inactivated, and assigned personnel were integrated with almost every organization at Dover AFB.

The wing's first female C-5 pilot, 1st Lt. Gayle I. Westbrook of the 3rd Military Airlift Squadron, flew her first operational mission on July 4, 1985. In 1987, Westbrook became the first female pilot in the 21st Air Force to be certified as an aircraft commander.

This all-female C-5 crew flew a seven-day European channel mission as part of the US Air Force Women's History Month celebration on March 28, 1988. The mixed crew of 17 members included women of the 436th and 512th Military Airlift Wings, plus two artists and a photographer from the Pentagon.

In 1986, the wing took delivery of its first Lockheed C-5B Galaxy aircraft, pictured here with a display of its airlift capabilities.

The wing transported the entire nine-plane US aerobatic team from Dover AFB to Cerney, England, without dismantling a single plane, in July 1986.

During frigid conditions at Dover, a C-5 prepares for an ironic mission to airlift Army National Guard personnel to an "arctic environment."

An armed guard is at the alert as a Lockheed C-5 Galaxy is loaded for Operation Just Cause, the invasion of Panama in December 1989.

Dover crews successfully dropped and test-fired a Minuteman I ICBM in 1974 and delivered a 40-ton superconducting magnet to Moscow in 1977 as part of a joint energy research program. The mission to Moscow earned the crew the Mackay Trophy for the most meritorious flight of the year. Missions to Zaire and another to the Soviet Union also earned Mackay Trophies for Dover captains and crews.

On December 9, 1978, members of the 436th Military Aircraft Wing assisted in the evacuation of 140 Americans from Iran to Dover AFB. In March 1989, wing C-5s delivered special equipment used to clean up the Exxon Valdez oil spill in Prince William Sound, Alaska.

Israeli soldiers guard a Dover C-5A during Operation Nickel Grass, a massive airlift mission during the Yom Kipper War of 1973. The Dover aerial port handled 1,807 tons of outbound cargo and 556 tons of inbound cargo involving some 364 missions. During Operation Nickel Grass, Dover's C-5s flew 71 missions, more than 2,000 hours, and delivered more than 5,000 tons of cargo. That operation is considered by many to have been the first real test of the C-5 aircraft.

Since their inception, the airlift wings at Dover have consistently provided humanitarian airlift in times of disaster and military airlift when the United States' forces were needed around the globe.

Deployed Dover AFB airmen are depicted here during Operation Desert Shield in October 1990. During Desert Shield, the wing flew approximately 17,000 flying hours and airlifted a total of 131,275 tons of cargo. Dover AFB became a major airlift hub and intermediate repair facility for C-5 aircraft participating in the operation.

Unidentified deployed Dover airmen are pictured in Afghanistan in 2002. Dover aircrews flew the first C-5 expeditionary airlift missions into Kandahar, Afghanistan, as well as landed C-5s into Baghdad International Airport for the first time since before the Gulf War.

Personnel worked around the clock preparing, loading, and transporting more than 450,000 tons of equipment and more than 142,000 personnel in support of the Global War on Terror.

The first C-17 Globemaster III aircraft, named *Spirit of the Constitution*, arrived at Dover AFB on July 2, 2007. The base has 13 of these aircraft assigned to the 436th Airlift Wing and the 512th Airlift Wing, providing a flying squadron and maintenance squadron to augment this mission. The C-17 is capable of rapid strategic delivery of troops and all types of cargo to main operating bases or directly to forward bases in the deployment area.

The "Super Galaxy" C-5M is a modification of the original C-5A/B series, designed to extend the lifetime of the aircraft and increase its reliability and capability. Dover is the host base for this modification program in progress. By the end of 2010, four C-5Ms were delivered, with more on the way.

Five

HERITAGE PRESERVED

Dover AFB is the home of the Air Mobility Command Museum, whose purpose is twofold: to preserve and present the history and heritage of both Dover Air Force Base and the Air Mobility Command. The museum is a part of the National Museum of the United States Air Force's field museum system. Air Mobility Command is a major command of the Air Force. Its mission is to deliver maximum war-fighting and humanitarian effects for America through rapid and precise global air mobility.

In 1986, then wing commander and later MAC/AMC commander Gen. Walter Kross expressed interest in starting an air museum at Dover. He tapped Mike Leister as museum director and Jim Leach as museum curator. The team launched the museum idea starting with a C-47. They began working on several projects at once in various stages of repair. By 1999, they had moved into their present location in the historic Hangar 1301.

During World War II, the 4146th Base Unit was involved in secret rocket development. The building complex where these covert military operations took place was Hangar 1301. From the 1950s to the 1970s, various fighter squadrons called the hangar home. In the 1990s, after restoration and placement on the National Register of Historic Places, Hangar 1301 was given new life as the home of the Air Mobility Command Museum.

Today, the museum has more than 20,000 square feet of interior exhibit space, a theater, museum store, library, image archive, artifact storage area, and administration offices. It features a commemorative park and, above all, a superb collection of military aircraft, specializing in transport and aerial refueling aircraft. It is a growing collection that at this writing contains some 27 aircraft; most are featured in the following chapter.

This book closes by honoring those who have given their lives for their country. Since 1955, the Dover AFB mortuary has processed the remains of the country's servicemen and servicewomen and honored their sacrifices. The Charles C. Carson Center for Mortuary Affairs is the largest in the Department of Defense and plays a vital role as a place of honor where the remains of DoD personnel killed overseas are received.

The roots of the Dover museum date to 1986, but the seed was planted in 1978 when *Shoo Shoo Shoo Baby* arrived on base from the Air Force Museum at Wright Patterson AFB. *Shoo Shoo Shoo Baby* was a B-17 bomber basket case. It began as an Air Force Reserve restoration project to restore the craft to wartime flying condition, an idea conceived by TSgt. Mike Leister.

Lt. Col. C.M. Hall and the crew of the 350th Bomb Squadron, 303rd Bomb Group stand beside a Boeing B-17 Flying Fortress named *Shoo Shoo Shoo Baby* in England on April 7, 1944. This airplane is one of more than a dozen various aircraft going by the name Shoo Shoo Baby. A similar museum airplane had been interned in Sweden after damage during a mission to Poland. After the war, it was modified as a passenger transport and as a photograph-mapping craft, flying for Sweden, Denmark, and France.

Arriving via a C-5 in 17 major pieces, the bomber was restored at Dover by the 512th Antique Aircraft Restoration Group, an organization of volunteers and community members. It took more than 10 years of extraordinary restoration efforts totaling more than 40,000 volunteer hours before it was finally airworthy. *Shoo Shoo Shoo Baby* made its first flight in more than 27 years in August 1988 and its last flight to the Air Force Museum in Ohio in October 1988.

The C-47A *Turf & Sport Special* undergoes aircraft maintenance during World War II. After the war, it was retired to a field in Pennsylvania where the shell was used as a training aid. That airplane, a C-47, was the first aircraft of the new Dover Air Force Base Historical Center.

The Air Mobility Museum began in 1986 with a single C-47A that was rejected as "beyond salvage" by other museums. Today, it stands immaculately restored, complete with D-Day invasion stripes, to look as it did when it served with the 61st Troop Carrier Squadron in World War II. Its extensive combat history is meticulously documented with actual photographs and memorabilia donated by former crew members.

Although produced too late to see combat in World War II, this B-17G, *Sleepy Time Gal* (serial no. 44-83624), saw extensive service in flight-testing missiles and drones. In 1957, it was retired to the Air Force Museum at Wright-Patterson AFB in Ohio. In 1989, it was given to Dover to replace the famous B-17G *Shoo Shoo Shoo Baby* that was restored over a 10-year period.

In 1933, Stearman Aircraft began production of the Kaydet and did not end production until 1945 after some 10,000 had been built in a variety of forms. The Kaydet was a rugged two-seat primary trainer for the military. It was the first plane that student pilots flew solo during their 60 hours of primary instruction. The PT-17 biplane trainer donated by Al Johnson, a local aerial sprayer, was restored using pieces from several aircraft and hand-fabricated replica parts.

The Air Mobility Command Museum's BT-13 Valiant (serial no. 42-1639) was the basic trainer most widely used by the US Army Air Force during World War II. Nicknamed "the Vibrator" by the pilots who flew it, the BT-13 was powered by a Pratt & Whitney R-985 engine. By the end of World War II, 10,375 BT-13s and BT-15s had been accepted by the Army Air Force.

The Douglas A-26 was a World War II attack aircraft used for level bombing, ground strafing, and rocket attacks. The A-26 entered combat over Europe in November 1944. By the time production halted, 2,502 Invaders had been built. The Invader fought in the Korean War and once again in Vietnam. The A-26 was redesignated the B-26 in 1948, thus creating everlasting confusion with the World War II Martin B-26 Marauder.

Dover's first strategic airlifter is represented by the single remaining C-54M (serial no. 44-9030), which was specially modified during the Berlin airlift for hauling coal. The Skymaster's restoration was also quite extensive and took several years. The inside shows examples of its World War II cargo and passenger configurations. The C-54 on display at the museum is the last surviving M model in existence. There were only 38 of this model manufactured.

The Flying Boxcar was developed by Fairchild Aircraft in the 1940s as a specialized military freight aircraft for the US Army. From the 1940s into the late 1960s, the C-119 was modified and redesigned as new technologies and uses evolved. The Air Mobility Command Museum boxcar (serial no. 10-870) is a G, the last major production model, powered with a Wright R-3350 engine. A total of 484 Flying Boxcars were built. They were used by the Royal Canadian Air Force as a firebomber and appear in the Richard Dreyfuss movie *Always*.

The first strategic long-range airlifter that performed yeoman service through two wars and nearly 25 years, the C-124, was affectionately known as Old Shaky. The C-124 was operational during the Korean War and also used to assist supply operations for Operation Deep Freeze in Antarctica. The C-124 was used to support troop build-ups in Europe during the 1961 Berlin Wall Crisis. It was capable of handling up to 74,000 pounds of cargo, such as tanks, field guns, bulldozers, and trucks. The aircraft could also be converted into a transport capable of carrying 200 fully equipped troops in its double-decked cabin or 123 litter patients. The Air Mobility Command Museum's Globemaster is one of only eight C-124s in existence and is the only surviving A model.

Conceived as an air transport for America's large missiles, the C-133 was designed to meet the requirements for the Air Force's Logistic Carrier Support System. The C-133 Cargomaster was developed by the Douglas Aircraft Company and was first flown on April 23, 1956. It was the largest turboprop transport ever to be accepted by the US Air Force. In 1958, C-133s began flying Military Air Transport Service air routes throughout the world, and two Dover-based C-133s established transatlantic speed records for transport aircraft on their first flights to Europe. The fleet of 50 aircraft proved itself invaluable during the Vietnam War, but fatigue problems led to their withdrawal from service in 1971.

TOTAL S·T·R·E·T·C·H
23.3 FEET

120"   160"

This Lockheed company photograph illustrates the same C-141A Starlifter aircraft before and after "stretching" to the C-141B configuration. The Air Mobility Museum has examples of both aircraft. Their C-141A (serial no. 61-2775) is the first one built. Their C-141B Starlifter (serial no. 64-0626) was the very last C-141 stationed at Dover AFB. It retired in February 1996.

In 1996, Amoco Corporation purchased a lot in Penndel, Pennsylvania, that contained a restaurant topped by a Lockheed C-121 Constellation (serial no. 4557) aircraft. Realizing the historical significance of the plane, Amoco offered the plane to the Air Mobility Command Museum. It was transported to the museum in December 1997 and is now completely restored. The Constellation was the first commercial transport plane to travel at 300 miles per hour and was the last of the great American propeller-driven airliners. In addition, Military Air Transport Services used a fleet of 70 C-121s from 1948 to 1967 that were similar to the one depicted here.

The C-7 Caribou (serial no. 63-9760) was flown to the museum in 1992, and as its past was traced it was found that the plane was stationed at Cam Ranh Bay, Vietnam, from 1969 to 1970. One of the museum's volunteers, Col. Bill Hardie (Retired) researched his flight records of the time he spent at Cam Ranh Bay and found that he and the plane were old buddies.

After serving in Vietnam, the museum's C-123 Provider (serial no. 54-658) went on to further distinguished service. After retirement from the US Air Force, it was picked up by the Department of State and was instrumental in the war on drugs in Peru. Because of its unique capabilities as a cargo transport plane and its ability to use unimproved landing strips in remote regions, the plane was nicknamed "El Burro" by Peruvians.

The Lockheed C-130 Hercules is a four-engine, turboprop-powered, tactical airlift aircraft capable of operating from austere airfields. More than 40 foreign countries as well as the US Air Force, Coast Guard, Navy, Marines, and Air National Guard operate C-130s. The Delaware Air National Guard continues to maintain a fleet of C-130Hs at nearby New Castle Airport. The C-130 on display (serial no. 69-6580) was retired from active duty on February 2, 2004, and made its final flight to the Air Mobility Command Museum.

Pictured is the cargo version of the KC-135E Stratotanker. The KC-135 provides the core aerial refueling capability for the US Air Force and has excelled in this role for more than 50 years. It also provides aerial refueling support to US Air Force, Navy, Marine Corps, and allied nations' aircraft. The KC-135 is also capable of transporting litter and ambulatory patients. This Air Mobility Command Museum's Stratotanker (serial no. 57-1507) was flown to Dover from the New Jersey Air National Guard.

A single HH-43 Huskie was assigned to Dover from 1959 to 1962. The Huskie was used primarily for crash rescue and aircraft firefighting. The H-43 Huskie set an altitude record of 10,000 meters and numerous rates-of-climb records. During the Korean and Vietnam Wars, the Huskie flew more rescue missions than all other aircraft combined and kept the best safety record of any US military aircraft.

The T-33 is still one of the world's best-known aircraft, having served with air forces of more than 20 different countries with some well cared for aircraft still flying today out of the more than 7,000 built. In the more than 55 years since its introduction, the T-33 has been flown to help train more jet pilots than any other training aircraft type. The Air Mobility Command Museum's T-33 (serial no. 52-9497) was stationed at Dover and used by Military Air Transport Service pilots for proficiency.

The C-9A, known as "Nightingale," was developed to fill the need for an Aero Medical Evacuation (Medevac) aircraft. The Air Force purchased 20 C-9As to replace older propeller-driven Medevac planes. The museum's plane (serial no. 67-22584) was the first C-9A delivered to the Military Airlift Command in 1968 and was retired from the Air Mobility Command in August 2005 after 37 years of outstanding service.

This photograph of the Air Mobility Command Museum's KC-97 is illustrative of the typical condition of the aircraft received. It gives one a sense of the magnitude of restoration needed, especially when contrasted against the finished result many thousands of volunteer hours later.

This Boeing KC-97L Stratofreighter was assigned to the Strategic Air Command in 1955 at Westover Air Force Base in Massachusetts. In 1965, it was converted to KC-97L status by the addition of two jet engines and transferred to the Tennessee Air National Guard. It is similar to the KC-97s based at Dover in the early 1960s with the 11th Air Refueling Squadron.

The Air Mobility Command Museum has an actual plane from the 95th Fighter-Interceptor Squadron that was stationed there in 1972. The Dart first flew in 1956, and a squadron of the delta-wing interceptors was stationed at Dover AFB with the 95th from 1963 to 1973. An all-weather interceptor known for its efficiency and ability to counter bomber aircraft up to 70,000 feet, the F-106A had a maximum speed of 1,525 miles per hour (Mach 2.3) and a range of 1,500 miles. It carried four Falcon missiles and one Genie nuclear rocket. Starting in 1972, the 106s were transferred to the 177th Fighter-Interceptor Group at Atlantic City, New Jersey, making the Dart the last type of fighter assigned to Dover AFB.

The Voodoo became the principle aircraft of the 98th Fighter-Interceptor Squadron stationed at Dover Air Force Base in the mid-1950s to mid-1960s. Its job was to defend Washington, DC, and the Eastern United States over the course of the Cold War. At any time, the 98th was ready to scramble into the air within five minutes. The Air Mobility Command Museum F-101 is displayed in the markings of the 98th Fighter-Interceptor Squadron from Dover.

The Air Mobility Command Museum's C-131 Samaritan has run the gamut. It started out as a staff plane for the Air Force Air University and ended its service as a South Carolina Air National Guard general's plane. It was also the museum's first "flyable" aircraft. This short- to medium-range transport was stationed at Dover Air Force Base in its T-29 version.

Better known as the Huey, the UH-1 Iroquois was obtained by Dover AFB for use as a load trainer. An Army version is depicted here in the 1960s. It has been repainted to represent an Air Force Huey used for medical evacuation, rescue missions, and administrative support. This helicopter is on display at the museum but it is not a part of the museum's collection.

The arrival of the remains of the Vietnam Unknown at Dover AFB is depicted here. The Port Mortuary is the largest in the Department of Defense and plays a vital role as a place of honor where the remains of DoD personnel killed overseas are received.

On May 28, 1997, wing officials renamed the Dover Air Force Base Port Mortuary the Charles C. Carson Center for Mortuary Affairs. This memorialization was in honor of Carson's 40-year tenure as director.

In 1955, the Aerial Port Mortuary responsibilities were transferred to Dover, and many Americans have become familiar with the base for its prominence and exceptional service in fulfilling that duty. To offer an incomplete list, the Port Mortuary has received the remains of casualties of the war in Vietnam, a number of plane and helicopter crashes involving military personnel, the mass suicide in Guyana, the attack on the Marine barracks in Beirut, Pan Am Flight 103, the USS *Iowa*, the Khobar Towers bombing, the 1998 US embassy bombing in Kenya, and the September 11 attack on the Pentagon.

The Charles C. Carson Center for Mortuary Affairs, a $30-million, 73,000-square-foot, state-of-the-art facility, became home to the mortuary in October 2004. The mortuary not only serves as the nation's sole port mortuary but is the largest mortuary in the DoD and the only one located in the continental United States.

A sailor honors the remains of a crewman from the bombed USS *Stark*. The Dover Port Mortuary served the USS *Cole* crew and the astronauts from the *Challenger* and *Columbia* disasters, in addition to the ongoing needs of conflicts around the world.

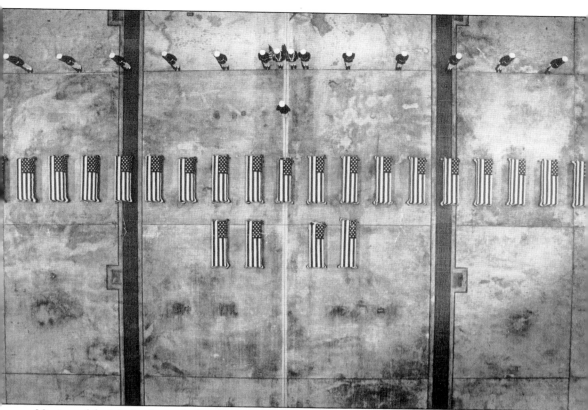

Victims of the Marine barracks bombing in Lebanon in 1983 are shown in this overhead photograph. Known as dignified transfer, this is the solemn movement of the fallen from arrival aircraft to the mortuary by respective service honor guards.

DISCOVER THOUSANDS OF LOCAL HISTORY BOOKS FEATURING MILLIONS OF VINTAGE IMAGES

Arcadia Publishing, the leading local history publisher in the United States, is committed to making history accessible and meaningful through publishing books that celebrate and preserve the heritage of America's people and places.

Find more books like this at
www.arcadiapublishing.com

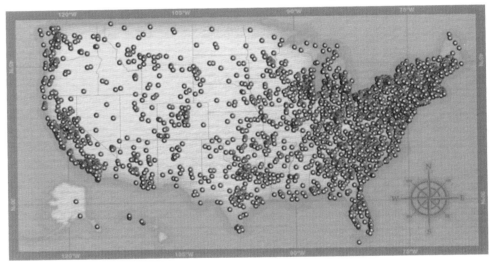

Search for your hometown history, your old stomping grounds, and even your favorite sports team.

MADE IN THE
USA